Terminal Park

TERMINAL PARK

POEMS BY
Richard Wakefield

ABLE MUSE PRESS

Able Muse Press

www.ablemusepress.com

Library of Congress Cataloging-in-Publication Data

Names: Wakefield, Richard, 1952- author.
Title: Terminal park : poems / by Richard Wakefield.
Description: San Jose, CA : Able Muse Press, 2021.
Identifiers: LCCN 2020003089 (print) | LCCN 2020003090 (ebook) | ISBN 9781773490687 (paperback) | ISBN 9781773490694
Subjects: LCGFT: Poetry.
Classification: LCC PS3623.A3566 T47 2021 (print) | LCC PS3623.A3566 (ebook) | DDC 811/.6--dc23
LC record available at https://lccn.loc.gov/2020003089
LC ebook record available at https://lccn.loc.gov/2020003090

Printed in the United States of America

Cover image: *Damning Dalmatian* by Rebecca Scholz

Cover & book design by Alexander Pepple

Able Muse Press is an imprint of *Able Muse: A Review of Poetry, Prose & Art*—at www.ablemuse.com

Able Muse Press
467 Saratoga Avenue #602
San Jose, CA 95129

To CMW, as always

Acknowledgments

I am grateful to the editors of the following journals, where many of these poems originally appeared, sometimes in earlier versions:

Able Muse: "Fellow Traveler," "Keepaway," and "The Orchard Keepers"

Bellowing Ark: "The True Miracle of the Loaves and Fishes"

Better Than Starbucks: "Annual Physical," "Dante's House," "Dry Season," "Gathering at the River," "Getting Current," "Hedonic Calculus," "Mortal Math," "The Nature of Things," "Night Visit," "Nothing to Fear," "Old Folks at the Rec Center," "The Plunge," "The Polaroid," "Spray Park," "Undivided," "Words as Weapons," and "Written in Despair"

The Buckeye: "Even the Disciples" and "The Heaven of the Senses"

Crosscurrents: "The Long Afterward"

Garo: "Sonata for Solo Cello" and "Willful Misreading"

Iambs & Trochees: "Terminal Park"

Life and Legends: "Subtle Math"

Light: "Driving Backwards" and "Uncle Owen's Essex"

Measure: "By Winter Light," "Old Windows," "Pilgrims," and "Re-Creation"

Pivot: "Forbidden Fruit"

The Road Not Taken: "To Market, to Market" and "Verses on Mutability, with a Line from Ecclesiastes"

Rose Alley Press Anthology: "Brought to Light," "Divergence," and "*The Gross Clinic*"

Terrain.org: "Spring Flood"

Trillium: "The Smell of Time"

Thanks also to the editors of *Life and Legends*, where "Gathering at the River" was republished; and to the editors of *Garo*, where "The Orchard Keepers" was republished.

Contents

II A Deeper Hunger

III A Quaking Belly

IV   Entanglements

V   A Further Range

Terminal Park

I Terminal Park

Terminal Park

"Terminal Park" reads the vine-covered sign
where junkies and drunks reach the end of the line.
Come morning the coroner's van threads its way
through under- and overgrowth gone to decay.
But this *was* a park once, the sweet countryside,
a Sunday adventure where people would ride
in the days of the streetcar, away from the grime
and the stench of the city, both ways for a dime.
The place wasn't named with sardonic intent;
to them the name literally said what it meant:
this was, after all, where the terminal was,
and the dactyl in "terminal" pleased them because
it mimicked the clickety-clack of the track
that lullabied babies to sleep going back.
And right in the center a marvel was set:
the engines were turned in a slow pirouette
on a platform that carried the giants with ease
in an arc of a hundred and eighty degrees.
But ironies happen. The auto age came
and abandonment wrought a new turn on the name.
The literal iron was scrapped and the place
was left unattended, a terminal case.
Now derelicts shiver by fires in the dark
with no return tickets from Terminal Park.

A Holdout

The farm held out against the sprawl
the modern age embraced
until its fence lines faced
three subdivisions and a mall.

At last, death left the farm unmanned,
the fields untilled, until
the heirs could break the will
and reap a fortune from the land.

While they worked deals the land grew dense
with alder, running vines,
and even seedling pines
behind the sagging wire fence.

Thus unproductive nature bloomed
perversely, for a time,
then yielded to prime
suburban lots, so smoothly groomed.

It's no use asking whether deep
in us there's such a place,
or if we've purged all trace
of what we can't afford to keep.

Tractor Laureate

The John Deere green has faded
to match the morning glory
tendrils that have braided
themselves in desultory
garlands deep among
the grease-black engine bay.
One loader arm is hung
like an iron espalier
in blossoms, white and belled.
The apparatus stands
at idle, softly held
by interwoven strands
that something unseen drives
among, within, about.
The hulk's outline survives
in what it tractored out.

Old Windows

The windows in an old house warp with age.
The world outside that filters through the glass
is like the printing on a rain-soaked page—
the old familiar garden, trees, and grass
that unremitting labor kept in order
now fluctuate and float in rippled light
that seeps and bleeds, obscuring every border.
No squint can squint confusion from your sight
and any move you make just makes it worse,
a vertigo of near-delirium.
Uncertain verticals—prompting perverse
horizons—angle in and out of plumb.
The madness settles down as darkness falls;
the page you gaze on fades to blank and black.
The old geometries of floor and walls
and ceiling, a small but safer world, come back.
But as you stand reflecting on the square,
the dark rewritten page gives back a face,
distorted out of recognition there,
that wavers ghostlike over empty space.

Undermined

Riddling tunnels undermine this town.
Intersecting, radiating, down
and down they maze their way away from light
pursuing heliophobic anthracite.
Nothing stirs down there these days unless
a rotted cross-brace snaps beneath the press
of countless tons of rock. Then in the street
above the people feel beneath their feet
the vaguest rumble, the slightest seismic shift,
as if the winches strained again to lift
their tons of coal through half a mile of earth.
But they know better. What's left there isn't worth
the cost to delve so deep and hoist so high.
The semi-trucks and freights that rattle by
the idle terminal where nothing stops
disturb abandoned houses and empty shops.
Sometimes at night when there's no breeze, a whiff
of incense rises from the dust, as if
some curious soul had pushed against the door
of a room that no one lives in anymore.

The Orchard Keepers

The scene that opened at their farmhouse door
that summer was of apple trees that spread
along the contours of the valley floor,
breeze bestirred and mottled rust and red.

It wasn't merely part of what they'd planned.
It was a sacred metaphor that meant
the bond between them, between them and the land,
and to the wind that bore the apple scent.

But airborne apple sweetness falls to must;
their elders could have told them what would come,
a storm of willful choices, gust on gust,
and hard results there is no turning from.

Between contending winds of will or fate,
or by some fatal blow combining both,
the paradise they labored to create
fell to snags and tangled undergrowth.

Written in Despair

She crests the hill between their farm and town
and surveys their west fifty in the sun.
The new-tilled soil glistens a richer brown,
but half the morning work remains undone.
At a furrow-end stands the abandoned plow,
like punctuation—a period? a dash?
a finish, or only a pause? She shades her brow
to read the message in the ruts that slash
across the tillage, as if a writer struck
his morning's labor in despair. The line
leads home where, in the yard, beside the truck,
the tractor clicks as it cools. She knows the sign.
If only she could strike the years she spent.
No lease or purchase should be so ironclad—
no earthly contract—as the sacrament
that keeps her throwing good years after bad.
Her pickup rattles across the cattle guard.
The house is silent, as if there's no one home.
She steers the tractor back across the yard
to finish the story written in the loam.

Forms and Forming

Do you recall the form sent from the bank,
the work of clerks, accountants, financiers,
an amortization table that filled the blank
of thirty formerly uncommitted years?
And then the house, with all those blanks to fill,
closets and cupboards, that white, unpictured wall,
no flowers on the kitchen windowsill,
the pair of empty bedrooms down the hall?
In filling in those blanks did we submit
to forms the world imposed on us? Did we
leave uncreated lives that didn't fit
the selves the forms intended us to be?
Or were we figures latent in the stone,
discovering forms inherently our own?

The Flesh Remembers

This afternoon the old man's fitful sleep
is haunted by the breath of new-mown lawn
that whispers, like a spirit on the deep,
of waking in a long-ago predawn.
His father's rumble shakes the bedroom wall:
"In heaven there'll be time enough to rest,
in this world we've got hay to bale and haul."
He hears the swallows flutter from their nest
beneath the eaves, as if they understand
that work comes first and last in this dark place.
He stirs and wakes and holds his calloused hand
against the sun that slants across his face.
There where sixty years of work are shown,
he reads his father's words made flesh and bone.

The Long Afterward

The ripe fruit she called *more than enough* now lies
wherever it falls, a feast for wasps and birds,
instead of doing for autumn's sauce and pies
and preserves for winter's chilly afterwards.

Afternoons, her grownup grandson comes
to see that she is up and out of bed,
and sees the trees, one each of peaches, plums,
and apples that she culled and harvested.

She wears a sweater on the warmest day
but opens a window to let the breeze waft through
with mingled scents of ripeness and decay.
"That's enough," she says. "That will do."

Spray Park

Some years it's August here before the snow
gives way to flowers on the mountainside.
So small a span is granted them to grow—
no more than sixty days of heat divide
the winters barely past and soon to come.
They bloom before the long white afterwards,
and blooming brings the things that buzz and hum,
and buzzing, humming things bring flocks of birds.
We sit on sun-warmed stones to rest our legs,
to drink, to eat our meal of bread and cheese.
In lowland parks a robin all but begs,
hops nearer, farther, pantomiming *please*.
But here, these tattered gray jays can't afford
the gaudy colors other birds display
and can't afford the risk of being ignored:
they swoop and strike and won't be shooed away.
The shortened spring and summer here that warms
their urgent avarice to fire, the same
that heats the insects into boiling swarms,
ignites the blooms in red and yellow flame.
From books we learned that this is called the course
of nature; in this interval from bud
to blank oblivion, we feel its force
alive and rising in our bones and blood.

Willful Misreading

A nurse log, rotted almost down to duff,
gave rise to Douglas firs in ragged rank,
as if some hand had set a fence of rough-
hewn posts along this rocky, root-bound bank.
By braided years, the river shifts its course
according to unseen necessities,
and swollen with the snowmelt turns its force
against the bank to undercut the trees.
Sometimes they topple and are borne away
in one dramatic, cataclysmic crash,
while others angle slowly, day by day,
to kiss their reflections with the merest splash.
These days the scene suggests a metaphor
that takes a willful blindness to ignore.

II A Deeper Hunger

The True Miracle of the Loaves and Fishes

Matthew 14:14–20

He didn't simply create more loaves and fishes.
That would be mere magic. Any fake
Messiah could mumble mumbo jumbo to make
the baskets swell until the crowd was fed.
He knew as no one in the multitude
that what they hungered for that day was not
to fill their bellies—though that was what they thought—
but sustenance and substance greater than food.
He passed the baskets, let the people look
inside and look within, and there they saw
their hearts were starved; they knew that to withdraw
mere food would starve them more. They all forsook
their own desire and passed the baskets on,
while those who'd hoarded food put theirs inside
until, behold, they all were satisfied
although unfed, their deeper hunger gone.

Even the Disciples

Mark, Chapter 9

They left their boats and nets and followed Him
without a backward glance, forsaking all,
and not because a host of seraphim
directed them, but merely at His call.
They saw how He revived Jairus's daughter.
They saw how He restored a withered hand.
They saw Him calm the sea and walk on water.

They saw and yet they failed to understand.
Their failure comforts us who are unsure,
since those who climbed Mt. Hermon's slopes and saw
the Lord transfigured in a light as pure
and radiant as God, blind with awe,
were still confused, for all that they had seen,
just what this "rising from the dead" could mean.

The Heaven of the Senses

Whatever pleasures heaven brings to hand,
I think it's texture that I'll miss;
no disembodied bliss compares to this—
the grain of wood, the grit of sand.

I treasure sound and sight and taste and smell:
breezes breathing in the eaves,
fallow fields going green,
the sourness of a Gravenstein,
the autumn must of mired leaves.
But heaven without touch would feel like hell.

Transcendent endless bliss would not be much
without the primal sense of skin on skin.
We make our higher earthbound heaven in
reciprocal indulgences of touch.

Dante's House

On a mid-December night, I went astray
in the streets of Florence, dark and serpentine,
an underworld of winding way on way.

Lost in the realm of Guelph and Ghibelline
I abandoned hope of finding my way back
by signs in undecipherable Florentine.

A swarm of Vespas ripsawed through the black
piazza spewing the sulfur stench of hell,
but by their bug-eyed lights I saw a plaque

in English and Italian, placed to tell
a lost soul this was Dante's house, and clear
and close I heard our duomo's vesper bell.

The church and poet told me I was near
the safety I had wandered from alone.
The night's despair began to disappear;

I lit upon a footpath I had known
by day and came full circle through the night
to see, across a square of cobblestone,
the steady beacon of our window light.

Selfie of the Artist as a Young Man

The church where I was baptized catches the sun
like Icarus. There's the cross, behind my ear.
The priest who baptized me and the elderly nun
who taught me my catechism and math appear
beside my forearm, extended where I hold
my phone to take the photo. There was sleet
that morning; this shifting Dublin day was cold
enough to freeze a wandering moocow's teat.
I wished I were in a smithy forging—well,
something, I don't know what, but someplace hot,
though not like that eternal Catholic hell
that punctuated every lesson they taught.
I uploaded this one as a Facebook post
with another of me and Nora on our bikes
beside Parnell's statue, a stately ghost
in weathered bronze, and got a dozen likes.

Gathering at the River

Where the creek is ponded up behind the weir
in Maltby's meadow stands the congregation
to baptize half a dozen youths and hear
Pastor Jackson's promise of salvation.

This humble backwoods creek and pond are now
the River Jordan Christ was baptized in,
as, robed in bed sheets, one by one they vow
to give their hearts to God and turn from sin.

A boy who was in last year's crop observes
a girl emerge, sees how from neck to knee
the sodden cotton clings to womanly curves.
A world-weary elder sees him see.

The old man knows that Jesus has their hearts
but Satan keeps his hold on other parts.

Pilgrims

"Another mile, another low-rent shrine,"
your seatmate mumbles. Half the tour group stays,
but you lurch down the aisle to get in line.
A bus you've been one stop behind for days
pulls out and you see weary faces pass
like pilgrims grimly bent on plodding on—
there's you, reflected darkly in the glass;
before you recognize yourself, you're gone.
Exhaust fumes spiral toward the overcast.
You see a peasant in the distance stop
his ox to let a tractor lumber past,
axle-deep in some anemic crop.
The toilet shelter reeks. You turn away
and shuffle with the line that snakes inside
the sanctum where some sooty mosaics portray
"creation myths," according to the guide.
The driver beeps. You decline to buy
a postcard, but from the corner of your eye
you glimpse a swath of tile rubbed clean, a blue
as undefiled as Eden's morning sky.

Verses on Mutability, with a Line from Ecclesiastes

I found a rundown storage shack that stood
where rows of fruit trees had been overrun,
hemmed in and held up by the cottonwood
and birches that obscured the orchard's sun.

The handmade *Keep Out!* sign was weather-streaked
in faded hunter green and nailed askew
above the gaping door. The hinges creaked
but seemed to croak "come in" as I passed through.

The smell of leaves outside gave way inside
to dust, where spider webs had claimed the place;
now knots of moths and flies hung mummified
and swayed as silk strands broke across my face.

A winter storm had torn away a square
of roof, allowing sun and seeds to seize
the spot beneath and start a forest there
of salal, grass, and tortuous, knee-high trees.

Men come and go but earth abides, they say,
to overgrow an orchard, and a shack.
If I should go but to return some day
I'd find no trace of them on coming back.

III   A Quaking Belly

Fellow Traveler

I'm five years old, a late-October night.
My father wakes me, takes me by the hand;
in robes and slippers we go outside to stand
on dew-chilled grass to see, high up, a light
that moves. And moves. It's 1957.
My father says the Russians have leapt ahead.
By building missiles instead of baking bread,
the godless souls have marred the face of heaven.
Although I'll come to question what I'm told
through shifting constellations of belief,
that strange word, "Sputnik," always brings a brief
but heart-deep stab, a remnant of the cold,
a vision of the new star, far and high,
that traced its arc against the silent sky.

Keepaway

The playground hosts a noontime game today.
They bait the fattest kid in school to chase
his lunch bag in a game of keepaway.
He lurches back and forth across the space
the crowd has cleared and has no breath to plead
with this boy, that boy, this boy, anyone.
His dignity is lost, he's losing speed,
despite their rhythmic taunt of *run-run-run!*
A practiced thrower makes the treasure sweep
just low enough to graze his fingertips
but higher than the boy could dream to leap.
He hefts his quaking belly, breasts, and hips
through graceless pirouettes around, around.

Far on the outskirts, with a loser's art,
the second-fattest boy in school has found
a place to be a part but stand apart—
until a high and errant toss descends.
Now in the small forever it will take
to fall his way, he vaguely comprehends
the weighty choice that falls on him to make.

Hedonic Calculus

A child who dropped her popcorn stands bereft
as Hecuba amid the wrack of Troy.
She feels no consolation in having left
a feast for crows that flock in raucous joy.

The birds in urgent ardor shove aside
their smaller ilk to peck the precious plunder.
More birds arrive. The girl retreats, wide-eyed.
An onlooker may feel her grief, but wonder:

Does some hedonic calculus prevail?
Would her enormous sorrow, weighed, out-sum
the crows' delight, to tip the pleasure scale,
or is there inherent equilibrium,

in which the gorging of so many maws
precisely balances the child's pain?
Or worse: to hear her sobs out-dinned by caws,
you'd think the net effect has been a gain.

Consider what the watching grown-ups feel.
Their sorrow for her sorrow complicates
the calculation of the commonweal
when factored with the countervailing weights.

Is her distress reduced in some small measure
by sympathy, or is their pain a plus
(or minus) that counts against the corvine pleasure?
The mathless crows feast on, oblivious.

Words as Weapons

One day at recess in second grade a kid
who tumbled from the monkey bars yelled, "Fuck!"
I'd never heard the word, or if I did
it hadn't stuck. We all were thunderstruck.
This was in the fifties, don't forget:
The f-bomb was atomic, though TV news
would leave unbleeped a racial epithet
to blaze from coast to coast in interviews.
An outraged teacher dragged the boy away
to Mr. Armstrong's office, by the ear.
But seeing my classmates galvanized that day
made an unintended lesson clear:
Whatever the rules of etiquette allowed,
a word can make you the center of a crowd.

Dry Season

By mid-July the lack of rain
has drained the green from knee-high grass.
Across the valley a verdant vein
still zigzags from a high crevasse,
a remnant of the vernal flood
against the brown. The pond it feeds
lies cupped in banks of sunbaked mud
as week by week the pool recedes.
The tracks of fox, raccoon, and deer
harden like sculpture in the sun.
And mine. They show that I've been here
a dozen times, the only one
to seek out water from this place.
The rain will come again in fall;
the rising water will erase
the record of our passing—all
the daily comings and goings, gone.
The grassland creatures will not think
in some far summer's thirsty dawn
to look for my tracks when they drink.

Riverside Camp

The dogs went wild at dawn,
and crawling from our tent
we found them baying on
the river bank. Some scent
or sound that found them from
the other side provoked
this pandemonium.

No matter how we stroked
or scolded them, the two
could not be calmed, but bared
their fangs at something through
the gloom. They barked and stared
as if the gates of hell
had opened and released
the atavistic smell
of some ungodly beast.

At last we glimpsed, among
the lodgepole boles and boughs
where witch-hair mosses hung,
a few bedraggled cows
that years ago had strayed
from someone's upstream farm.

Was this then what had made
the dogs raise their alarm?

It must have been, for when
they faded in the pines
the barking slowed and then
became uneasy whines.

Those feral cows had set
the dogs to frenzied fear.

The dogs had sensed a threat
in creatures once so near
their own domestic place,
and something stirred their hearts
when they awoke to face
their primal counterparts.

Spring Flood

In early spring the snowpack melts and floods
the lowland farms, leaving higher spots
where stolid cattle crowd and chew their cuds
impassively in ever-tighter knots.

The cattle stare their unreflective stare
at gnarled uprooted trees and sawmill logs
and bloated creatures from upstream somewhere,
distorted forms that could be calves or dogs.

From time to time the chaos coursing past
brings something swimming to the makeshift ark,
a muddy skunk, raccoon, or possum cast
by chance above the wavering water mark.

Newcomers take what space the space allows,
constrained to keep their brief, uneasy peace
with wary arabesques among the cows
and watch their ill-assorted tribe increase.

The beasts of farm and field, forced to share,
are unified by what divides around
their rain-soaked realm, dimly unaware
as bit by bit they lose their common ground.

Approaching Dark

On foot a half a mile from home
and half an hour from dawn he stops.
There's Galileo's starry dome,
a constellated arch that drops
to meet the bay immured in cloud.
That roiling bank of blankness drifts
across the streetlamps like a shroud,
obscures the spark each lamppost lifts
like stars that set by slow degrees.
As one by one the lights go dim
then flicker out, he plainly sees
the rising dark approaching him.

The Work of Darkness

Beneath the windrow trees he found them dead
where he had come to scythe the August grass:
birds—no, parts of birds, a wing, a head,
a mutilated breast at every pass.
Their kind or number the boy would never know,
so torn and scattered, as if an airborne flock
were blown to pieces, struck a mortal blow
beyond the speed and strength of any hawk,
and left uneaten here. What bird of prey
would waste its kill? The rot his blade revealed
was dark and vile against the sweet decay
of last year's leaves and this year's clover field.
The boy was only ten, and in the dim
demonic light, made darker by the glare
outward, the senseless slaughter weighed on him
and drove him out to uncorrupted air.
The harvest done, he came back to that place
to grasp his first of countless mysteries.
He found the ants and flies had left no trace
of stench to taint the rising autumn breeze.

The Plunge

Two dozen frightened eight-year-olds ascend
the ladder to the platform, where they creep
across or run with wild bravado, leap,
and plummet dumbly to the pool's deep end.

In this, the last ordeal of PE class,
I feel as if the ladder rungs are glue.
I can't look down, and looking up, my view
is Gary Sexton's skinny, trunk-clad ass.

Teddy Kirk, below me, stares in fear
at mine—the pucker too, for all I know.
The splashes resonating from below
grow distant even as they're growing near.

The caustic chlorine rising on a wave
of humid air enwreathes me in its fire,
and whispers tauntingly, "Higher! Higher!
It isn't any deeper than a grave!"

Our terror isolates us. We're alone,
and yet united by a common thing,
all joined in fear, like prayer beads on a string,
each bound to take the plunge inert as stone.

Then having leapt and lived, we feel we're blest
and vastly changed in such a fleeting time.
A world away, we watch the stragglers climb,
unbaptized souls so near their final test.

Summer Work

The old man down the road sold homemade wine.
He paid us local boys a dime a pound
for berries, ripe for shaking from the vine,
that overgrew uncultivated ground.
When other kids had gleaned the fruit at hand,
I propped the sprawling brambles with a board,
and crawling deep inside where I could stand,
was master of an untouched treasure hoard.
Our Sunday school teacher told us how
the vines and trees in Eden reached to place
their fruit in Adam's hands, the highest bough
and lowest bush bestowing boundless grace.
But blinking against the glare that stabbed my eyes,
bee-stung, scratched, and sunburnt, slick with sweat,
I knew I was as far from paradise
as any (mostly) sinless boy could get.
I counted up: a heaping bucket times
ten cents a pound, like I was keeping score.
That year I sold my summer days for dimes.
I don't remember what I spent them for.

To Market, to Market

At thirteen I was big enough to man
a truck at harvest time. It took strong arms
to steer the rutted gravel road that ran
to the railhead past a dozen miles of farms.
While smaller neighbor boys I knew were stuck
with children's chores when even in their teens,
I pulled a cloud of dust behind my truck
and saw them pulling weeds and picking beans.
If you can swagger sitting down, I did.
I gunned the engine, shifted gears, and thought
I surely was the envy of any kid
at stoopwork in his mother's garden plot.
A few short months I drove the countryside
perched high and mighty in a truck that bore,
whatever else, a bumper crop of pride
that I would never find a market for.

Micro and Macro

In mid-December on a warm
and rainless day, a sudden swarm
of gnats, a cloud of chaos, boils
with aimless energy, and roils
above the pond that didn't freeze
last night. Their frantic dance will squeeze
within the span of one day's heat
a life's essential course complete,
a universe of births, of quests
for mates, of deaths. This plague of pests
arises with the warmth and thrives,
then drops aside. We see our lives
in theirs, of course. Who stops to swat
away the swarm without a thought
of how like ours is their brief span?
To them we are gargantuan,
so huge our merest movements take
what must seem years, but still they make
us see ourselves in them, writ small.
Through swarm and swirl, rise and fall,
these mites that draw our animus
don't see themselves writ large in us.
Between a human and a gnat,
the great distinction lies in that.

Undivided

A blur of black Lab rockets off the dock
to hit the water ten feet out and cast
a cloud of crystals skyward in a shock
of broken rainbows whirling from the blast.

The dog desires no greater good in all
the world than this: to run and leap and swim
so wholly focused on a rubber ball
that bobs away on waves ahead of him.

He closes on it with a final surge
and arcs his course to home in on a boy
who's waiting on the bank, where he'll emerge
as fifty pounds of single-minded joy.

In years of emptiness and artifice
the man the boy becomes will think of this.

Arc of Blue, Arc of Blue

Morning fog muffles the breakers and hides
the ocean lying west, the woods to the east.
Today at one of the season's lowest tides
the water lies half a mile's damp-gray at least
from where he pitched his tent behind a dune.
No point in trudging to see what can't be seen
and what the cosmic clock will bring him soon
enough. His map promises him a ravine
and trail ascending the Coast Range and, with luck,
into the sun—though in his way, there lies
the asphalt four-lane like a ruler struck
across the contours, without a curve or rise
or fall. He times the tide of traffic: a few
artful strides put him among the trees;
more strides put the highway roar behind.
High in undulating topologies
he sees the arc of blue he came to find.
On a strangely smooth stretch of trail he scrapes
the muddy duff away with his walking stick,
releasing the scent of primal forestscapes
and revealing, beneath a blanket two inches thick,
a concrete road and the ghost of a center line—
the old coast highway, meandering through the fall
and rise of the land, now cracked and crazed by pine
and cedar roots but serving, after all
these decades, as a path for elk and deer—
and him. He follows as it climbs and turns

until a hilltop opens on the clear
Pacific where the line of breakers churns.
The ocean he turned his back on hours ago
pulses in sunlight against the curve of sand.
He studies the long arc of the beach below,
as graceful as the lifeline on his hand.

Subtle Math

Through the mirror of this alpine lake
a flash of silver leaps—like that!—
to take to air and take
a morsel of a gnat.

My shutter finger flicks a mite too slow,
my camera catches empty air
and rippled lake to show
that something happened there.

The wavering inverted peaks grow still—
then suddenly, another catch
my human speed and skill
are too evolved to match.

It's hard to see what math can justify
the fish's effort, all in all,
to thrust its bulk so high
to catch a bug so small.

Survival's long unbroken chain has taught
the fish that less plus less is more—
and, unlike me, it caught
what it was aiming for.

An Atomist Whispers through
the Roar of a Waterfall

The autumn rain and early melting snow
have swollen the falls to twice their summer flow.
Against the white and gray
of roiling clouds of spray
the sunlight fractures in a shimmering bow—

an arc of color—violet, indigo, blue,
each shading to and from its neighbor hue
too subtly to define
a strict dividing line.
The whole admits no part or partial view.

Democritus, were he here, would insist
that we and it and everything exist
suspended above the void,
created and destroyed
in random interplays of light and mist.

Today we click a picture and ignore
the whispered memento mori beneath the roar.
As form and chaos churn,
for now we will not turn
from this diverting scene we came here for.

Re-Creation

The mud that took my boot prints yesterday
still holds them as a record that I passed.
Some archeologist may come this way
ten thousand years from now and make a cast,

immortalize them on a plaster slab
and study them on her computer screen.
Amid the wonders of her future lab
she'll ponder what the symbols "Vibram" mean.

She may not recognize it, but she'll find
the record of a fracture poorly knit—
see here, the left foot's slightly misaligned,
and notice how the right heel drags a bit.

Will she assume that all mankind was flawed
and all our species shared my lack of grace?
Imagine me, become a paltry god,
my image used to recreate my race!

I hope, though, if my passing leaves a sign,
if only boot prints frozen into stone,
the faults are recognized as solely mine,
all mine, one man's mnemonics etched in bone.

IV   Entanglements

A Sun-Warmed Spot

He's walking past the open door
when something inside makes him glance
into the room, where years before,
his daughter slept. A luxuriance
of rumpled blankets used to keep
the imprint of the absent girl;
today the cat that loved to curl
around her pillow lies asleep,
as if she'd risen moments ago.
He stands there, gazing, stopped mid-pace,
to see the sun that slants below
the blinds to warm the empty place.

Driving Backwards

He bought a car when he retired
just like the ones that he admired
in high school, like the cool guys had.
His wife says, *Fine*, and doesn't add,
her date for junior prom drove one.
Well, she thinks, what's done is done;
they didn't know each other then.
She's too aware how fragile men
can be about a thing like that.
But riding beside him where she sat
beside that boy she feels the past
beside her coming back, and fast.
He dated her their junior year,
reached second base in second gear
and later in the drive-in's dark
reached third, and then stole home in Park.
She feels a long-forgotten thrill
recalling how he groped until
she helped him get her bra unclasped—
and things he much more quickly grasped.
A quick glance at the back seat shows
the place she lost her pantyhose
that night, and that's not all, by far.
Her husband proudly drives the car
completely unaware, she's sure,
of where the car is taking her.
That night it seems as if the cold

dead hand of habit doesn't hold
them quite so tightly; even though
it's only been a week or so
since they made love, they're at it now
in ways they had forgotten how,
indulging every sharpened sense.
They're sixty in experience
but seventeen again, entwined,
adventurous and rubber-spined.
Is he so vainly masculine
he thinks he knows what's gotten in-
to her? No point explaining it
if both enjoy the benefit
of his nostalgic automobile.
She can't help thinking how the wheel
of time turns unexpectedly
to carry us to places we
believed we had been driven from.
Perhaps he too was back in some
ideal scene of high-school love
that he has never told her of.
The past is past, indeed, and yet
some things our bodies don't forget.

Forbidden Fruit

We saw no angel with a flaming sword
to turn us back: a gate, a fading sign
that said *Keep Out*—so easily ignored
when Eden lay before us. The scent of pine
and cedar led us by the nose: Come In!
We crossed the line, we took the grassy path
to reach a sunny glade. The primal sin
we reenacted there called down no wrath
on us, unless one counts the tender welt
some nettles left imprinted on my ass,
a paltry pain for the pleasure that we felt
in delighted dallying on the dappled grass.
Our children wonder what we smile about
whenever we see a sign that says *Keep Out*.

Old Folks at the Rec Center

At recreation time the seniors come
to do a two-step relic from the age
of Fred Astaire. The bare gymnasium
sways to Mary Ford and Patti Page;
the jukebox used to play them for a dime.
The couples shuffle through "How High the Moon."
A girl from Parks and Rec counts out the time
and counts the minutes until she's off at noon.

With moves as finely grooved as a seventy-eight,
one pair defies their aching knees to twirl
in cautious arabesques. They recreate
their courtship ritual as boy and girl,
swinging toward each other, then away,
as giddy as their reckless yesterday.

The Polaroid

The lady down the street whose husband died
last year was sorting through his books and found
a half a dozen volumes to set aside
for me—some Twain, some James—leather-bound
editions, not so much to read as show.
Okay by me. I hadn't much enjoyed
The Portrait of a Lady years ago.
But inside I found a faded Polaroid:
a lovely woman, nude, and in her eyes
the love reflected at the man who took
the picture. It was easy to recognize
the lady who had given me the book.
The title was his trick to help recall
the sixty-year-old photo pressed in there.
Did she remember? It isn't, after all,
a thing you want discovered by an heir,
but neither is it something you would burn,
nor something you forget the wonder of.
What shame is there if someone else in turn
should glimpse this fragile relic of their love?

Brought to Light

The wind tore through on trash-collection day
and scattered secrets up and down the street.
Our private lives lie jumbled, indiscreet,
though what belonged to whom is hard to say.
An upwind neighbor's Playboy playmates pose
in Mrs. Jones' begonias brazenly.
Losing Lotto tickets deck a tree
like anemic leaves where disappointment grows.
Intimate prescriptions and bills past due
bear names, though none the finder recognizes.
And what if he did? The catalog of vices
shows us almost nothing unique or new.
What's strange is our capacity for shame
when what we strive to hide is all the same.

Intimate Strangers

At coffee hour after church, we met
a couple from the town that we came from,
a thousand miles away. We say *It's some
coincidence*, but more unravels yet:
comparing places, names, and dates, we learn
that her first husband's first wife's college flame
was . . . me. We chuckle, shake our heads, exclaim
Small world! Then, at loose ends, we quickly turn
to small talk: real estate, the traffic mess.
Our linkage in this genealogy
of lovers seems indelicate, yet we
(though silently) can't help but try to guess
what intimate impressions might remain
imprinted on strangers along the daisy chain.

Entanglements

A man and woman leave a room. She shuts
the door on tangled syntax, ands and buts
and either-ors, on tangled sheets and cries,
on tangled tongues and limbs and lives and lies.
Their ragged skein has found a denouement
today that neither he nor she foresaw.
They turn—he left, she right. She takes the stair
and he the elevator down to where
they thread their way as strangers through the knot
of strangers in the lobby, slack or taut,
who see no tie between them. Now their tense
is past. Now no one anywhere will sense
the scents of his cologne, of her perfume,
on her, on him, or mingled in that room.

Rhetoric

His middle-class suburban house and yard
and her blue-collar rental rowhouse past
were far apart, but love has scant regard
for trivialities of social caste.

One day "we *pluribus unum*, babe," he joked.
She didn't get it. He explained. She smiled
but didn't laugh. The awkward exchange provoked
a standoff. But love is love. They reconciled.

In private he thought the way she spoke was quaint,
and it wasn't as if he didn't know what she meant.
In public, though, he drew the line at "ain't"
and double negatives and "should have went."

His public "she and I" for "me and her"
were fine, but when they were alone he said
not "who" but "whom." What was sillier
than hoity-toity talk like that in bed?

At last with "snob" and "hick" their dissonance
confirmed it takes more kinds of intercourse
than one to keep a storybook romance
from ending in a grammar-book divorce.

Sonata for Solo Cello

The meadow lay as if inside a cup
with wooded hillsides rising to the brim.
And I heard music. A cello. Looking up,
I scanned the trees while music like a hymn
cascaded down in braided streams to pool
around me in the humid August air.
I knew there was a summer music school
nearby, and guessed the unseen player there
was playing hooky in the cedar shade,
and playing Bach in fluid baritone.
I paced the meadow out and back but stayed
in hearing of that grace from some unknown
creator, somewhere out of sight, who bowed
unmindful of the blessing he bestowed.

The Smell of Time

Sizzling French fries scent the evening breeze;
the wind tonight is from the Dairy Queen.
This afternoon it smelled of melting cheese
and garlic: Bob's Italian Quick-Cuisine.
This morning early-rising folk could sniff
the ersatz maple from the Pancake Palace.
Later tonight we'll catch a tempting whiff
of apple pie that wafts from Chez Alice.

In years past, north was from the cedar mill,
and south, in fall, was Maltby's fresh-cut hay.
The east was cow manure from Thrasher's Hill,
and west was salt and seaweed from the bay.
From year to year the breezes slack and swell
to place us in a shifting world of smell.

V   A Further Range

Stops Me Dead

My year of being sixty-six is past,
or *under my belt*, my father used to say,
and *days are long but years fly by so fast*,
and *while we're busy living, life slips away.*
He died too young. By now, though, he'd be gone
to settle up the score—as gone, that is,
as anyone can be whose words go on
surprising me, and in a voice like his.
At times it *stops me dead* to hear his tone,
inflections, pauses, *natural as can be*,
as if they're mine, as if they're *bred in the bone.*
I breathed them in, and now they're part of me.
These days I wonder who he got them from,
and who will echo them in years to come.

Getting Current

He must have heard a grownup say,
"We're getting current." That's the way
in later years he thought of it.
One night a neighbor's barn was lit
by stark electric light, so clean
it made the muted kerosene
look smudged and yellow. Driving back
from town along the narrow track
of gravel ruts, his father at
the wheel, the seven-year-old sat
in silence, and turned his head to watch
the glowing barn behind a swatch
of windbreak willows along the road
that made it flicker, as if in code,
now on, now off, a message beamed
from some bright time ahead. It seemed
to say that life would change and change—
and change. For now, the new-lit grange
proclaimed an end to early night.
Before the month was out, the light
came on inside their milking shed.
"Work first, then play," his father said,
as if it were frivolity
for people in a house to see
their way upstairs and down, to read
a book, to dress, without the need
to burn a smelly, smoky wick.

His mother's protests did the trick;
from pole to pole the line progressed
from shed to barn to house. The rest,
as people say, is history.
The rural folk at last were free
of living and working by the sun.
And that, they found, was only one
of many blessings. TV soon
would bring these rural folk the boon
of never feeling quite content.
And that's what "getting current" meant.

Surgery by the Numbers

Before they took the tumor out
they put him out, subtracting soul
from flesh so they could go about
their higher math, divide the whole
he was into the parts he'd be.
They multiplied his years, they said.
How much? He'd have to wait and see.
Meanwhile, in his hospital bed,
enhanced with stitches, tubes, and gauze,
he pondered what it means to gain
by losing, baffled by the laws
of medicine that cure through pain
and wrought this lessened self of his.
But he's alive. Or someone is.

Heredity

The sonogram gives us a week-by-week
uncertain view of you as you become.
We squint and analyze the latest peek,
debating who your nose and chin come from.
We dig out dusty albums to compare
your mother's pictures with what's on our screens
and swear we see a true resemblance there,
as if we've solved the mystery of genes.
Your father's parents do the same and find
his newborn image drawn in yours—no doubt—
and we concede the lines are intertwined
in knots no mortal eye can ravel out.
You'll grow to grow impatient, hearing us
exclaim how much of you derives from who;
we'll slowly come to grasp what's obvious
to you—that you are no one else but you.

Uncle Owen's Essex

When Uncle Owen went to World War Two
he parked his Essex out behind the shed
and put it on blocks, washed and waxed it, bled
the brake lines, drained the oil, and finally drew
a tent tarp over it, as if to tuck
it in. And there it sat. When he came home,
like everyone else he wanted speed and chrome,
not mid-Depression bland. He had no luck
at selling it, and couldn't give it away
unless he got it back in running shape.
Why bother? So without a dent or scrape
it sat for forty years, until one day
his grandson, my cousin Mike, discovered it.
He'd sneaked out back to have a smoke, but dropped
his match in wonder. To cruise the newly blacktopped
rural roads, not to have to sit
like a child beside his mother at the wheel!
A hint or two, and Owen, at sixty-five,
got it running and taught him how to drive.
The Essex had a subtle sex appeal
that wasn't lost on Mike, and neither on
the girl he dated and in time would wed.
The ancient Essex was slow, and yet it sped
the two across the unseen Rubicon
dividing youth from age. Now we can draw,
as Owen did, a general lesson: the wheel
will turn, and things gone out of style reveal
a charm and value nobody foresaw.

Night Visit

At two or three a.m. the aid car screams
through Golden Acres, where everyone's in bed
by nine. The wailing echoes in their dreams.
It's loud enough, they joke, to wake the dead.
One man back in bed after pissing, again,
lies awake and hears it thread the maze
of streets. He does a roll call of the men
he golfs with Tuesdays, Thursdays, and Saturdays:
one's X-rays show sclerotic arteries,
one's watch reminds him when to take his pills,
one's breathing has become a gurgling wheeze,
one's ruddy vigor masks pernicious ills.
And he himself, his LDL is high,
though not enough for statins, they say, not quite.
The siren in the distance passes by
and leaves his street in silence for tonight.

The Gross Clinic

after Thomas Eakins

(surgery: *from the Greek for* hand *and* work)

The scalpel, wound, and pencil glimmer bright
with lurid red that draws the viewer's gaze
across a flat expanse of somber grays.
Eakins puts himself to Gross's right,
making the artist and surgeon counterparts.
Their hands display the same precision grip
to yield their implements, the scalpel tip
and pencil point engaged in equal arts.

Between them, hands distorted into claws,
a woman throws her arm across her eyes—
the patient's mother. She personifies
the fragile human anguish Eakins draws
but Gross cannot allow himself to see,
a sense too deep to probe with surgery.

Annual Physical

It starts the year your doctor says, "Let's run
some tests on this. It may be nothing. Still . . ."
Every year till now your checkup was done
after you left the office and paid the bill.
This year there's more to pay. Maybe a lot.
Not least your sense of being someone apart
from clinics, prescriptions, lists of things you're not
supposed to do. It may not be your heart,
but then again, it is. At night you hear
it thumping as you never have before
and never had to, whispering in your ear,
"It may be nothing. It may be nothing. Or . . ."
The tests come back. You're fine. And yet you feel
a mortal wound that will not fully heal.

A Moment's Distraction

A week ago, at thirty-one degrees,
he saw the garden fenceposts etched in rime.
Now he's out here on his aching knees
to clear the season's weeds for planting time.
His wife told him this morning she would wait
for warmer days, as he laced up his boots,
but he hears the screen door slam, and then the gate,
and now she stoops among the vagrant shoots.
He thinks of Sunday school, how Adam and Eve
had perfect harmony before the fall,
how a serpent plotted to deceive
the simple couple into losing it all.
He laughs to think the serpent's work is done:
his knees, his back—they feel like, well, like hell.
He thinks they two beneath the feeble sun
are in the course of things a crop as well.
His laughter makes her ask, "What is it, dear?"
It sobers him to realize they're cursed
to bear a paradox: this year, next year,
some year one of them will be the first
to die, and he would pray that it be he
to spare himself the grief of losing her,
except he knows how great her grief would be
in losing him. A puzzle. The one thing sure
is that it will be solved. His hands are veined
and gnarled, grown old, as things mortal must;
with this labor in the dirt, they're stained

and well along their way of dust to dust.
She prods him in the ribs and asks again.
Is that the place once, so long before,
a rib was taken? He laughs again. And then
he says, "A moment's distraction, nothing more."

Divergence

He calls me when he's had too much to drink
at three a.m. Behind his voice I hear
a bottle kiss a glass with a stuttering clink.
He likes to talk about our junior year.
He talks of far more girls than I recall,
more staggering home at dawn, more missing class.
I nod. It was the sixties, after all;
I let the most unlikely stories pass.
We didn't see it then, the great divide
ahead, but who at twenty-one foresees
how whimsically the gods or fates decide
the twisting courses of our histories?
My number wasn't called. His was. His war,
my college took us down divergent streams.
He calls my number when he's grasping for
the strength to swim against his troubled dreams.
And so our one-way conversation goes,
these half-invented fantasies of his,
across the years and miles, as if to close
the gap between what might have been and is.

Nothing to Fear

There's nothing to fear. "Nothing," his mother said.
She held him, and when he grew too big to hold,
she sat beside him, smoothed his brow, and told
him, Nothing in the closet or under the bed;
nothing in the swaying trees that cast
their shadow limbs across his bedroom floor;
nothing in the empty house next door
that stares through glassless eyes as he walks past.
He didn't hear the strange foreshadowing,
the turn her words would take, but now he sees
the nothing in the empty house, the trees,
the nothing in anything, in everything,
the nothing coming closer year by year,
the promised nothing he has grown to fear.

The Nature of Things

The dozen horses make a writhing knot
against this afternoon of windblown sleet.
Driven to preserve their vital heat
they nose and jostle for the inmost spot.
If we had thought the storm would reach this height
we would have brought them in this morning—instead
we'll slog into a muddy winter night
to get the last one trailered, stalled, and fed.
For now my pickup cab is warm and dry.
Through a quarter-inch of windshield glass
I see the chaos swirling down the sky
to blast the horses' involuting mass.

Lucretius says they're particles in flux
from form to form, and so's the storm, and I'm
involved, I guess, as I wait for the trucks
and watch the wipers measure off the time.

Last Harvest

Out in the yard this autumn afternoon
he sees a bucket's worth of plums are strewn
among the brittle, reddened leaves brought down
by last night's wind. It bared the trees from crown
to bole but broke no limbs, and gave these plums,
a windfall harvest before the winter comes.

He plods. His flattened shadow flits ahead
then stands upright against the garden shed
and seems to pause to point at something there—
some summer-sun-warped boards that need repair.
(He feels a nudge about what shadows know,
connected somehow with the radio
that cast a red tinge on the whitewashed wall
behind it—something he can't quite recall.)
Recalled to here and now, he pushes the door
and finds he's forgotten what he's looking for:
those grating hinges—oil? The sun behind
his back shines on the workbench to remind
him it's the hammer, shrouded with a year
of dust and spider webs, that brought him here.

Something in its old familiar weight
gives him the ballast and balance to concentrate
his scattered study on the task at hand.
He bangs the nails in place, pauses to stand
beside his shadow on the wall, full-height,
and makes a last survey by fading light,
satisfied with what he's done today,
forgetting the plums, the odor of decay.

Mortal Math

Unborn, you're innocent of numbers now,
so I will do the math. In eighteen years
you'll graduate; if luck and genes allow
a normal span for me, then it appears
I could be more or less alive to see
that day. I'll be a specter in a chair
while everybody stands, deferring to me,
annoyed at my befuddled presence there.
I'm not afraid of age, I hope, nor fear
the only end of age, but hate to think
that image of me will crowd out, year by year,
the real me, growing as I shrink
to little, less, and nothing. I'll see all
your childhood, growing up and flourishing;
when you think back on me, you will recall
a hulk *sans eyes, sans taste, sans everything.*

By Winter Light

An old man at his kitchen window sees
by winter light, beyond a rough-hewn wall,
now held by weeds and skeletons of trees,
the garden gone untended since the fall.
Hard to see among the mud and moss
and rampant tansy tainted yellow-brown,
a tiny dun-gray bird flits quick across
his narrow view, back and forth, then down
to earth to peck at specks. For all it tries
against its beak it takes so few to eat—
the old man marvels that such a meager prize
can stoke the fist-sized spark of vital heat.
It flutters up the thorny hedge and skips
from vine to branch to probe the dark decay.
The old man tries his tongue and teeth and lips
against some words: *sparrow? swallow? jay?*
Once, the words he needed simply came
and bound themselves to creatures, one by one,
but now the bird flies off without a name,
as if some earthly knot has come undone.

Last Tasks of Summer

The roofers wage a September campaign.
Their Saturday-morning labor
wakes a drowsy neighbor
as they outpace the forecast rain.

Along the pitch they bang down sheets
of imbricated shingles.
Their gunshot tattoo mingles
with leaf blowers blaring along the streets.

Leaves to heap and shingles to nail—
no one is complaining,
and after it starts raining
the winter silence will prevail.

Today will tell if they have won
a narrow victory.
Their bustle speaks to me
of all that I've left unbegun.

Richard Wakefield earned his PhD in American literature from the University of Washington and has taught college humanities for forty-two years, thirty-five of them at Tacoma Community College. For over twenty-five years he reviewed poetry, fiction, and literary biography for the *Seattle Times*. His first book, *Robert Frost and the Opposing Lights of the Hour* (Peter Lang Publishing), was a study of Frost's poetry in the context of his life and times. His first collection of poems, *East of Early Winters* (University of Evansville Press), won the Richard Wilbur Award. His second collection, *A Vertical Mile* (Able Muse Press), was short-listed for the Poet's Prize. His poem "Petrarch" won the Howard Nemerov Sonnet Award. He and his wife, Catherine, have been married forty-eight years and have two daughters, two sons-in-law, and two grandchildren.

ALSO FROM ABLE MUSE PRESS

Jacob M. Appel, *The Cynic in Extremis: Poems*

William Baer, *Times Square and Other Stories;*
New Jersey Noir: A Novel;
New Jersey Noir (Cape May): A Novel;
New Jersey Noir (Barnegat Light): A Novel

Lee Harlin Bahan, *A Year of Mourning (Petrarch): Translation*

Melissa Balmain, *Walking in on People (Able Muse Book Award for Poetry)*

Ben Berman, *Strange Borderlands: Poems; Figuring in the Figure: Poems*

David Berman, *Progressions of the Mind: Poems*

Lorna Knowles Blake, *Green Hill (Able Muse Book Award for Poetry)*

Michael Cantor, *Life in the Second Circle: Poems*

Catherine Chandler, *Lines of Flight: Poems*

William Conelly, *Uncontested Grounds: Poems*

Maryann Corbett, *Credo for the Checkout Line in Winter: Poems;*
Street View: Poems; In Code: Poems

Will Cordeiro, *Trap Street (Able Muse Book Award for Poetry)*

Brian Culhane, *Remembering Lethe: Poems*

John Philip Drury, *Sea Level Rising: Poems*

Rhina P. Espaillat, *And After All: Poems*

Anna M. Evans, *Under Dark Waters: Surviving the* Titanic*: Poems*

Stephen Gibson, *Frida Kahlo in Fort Lauderdale: Poems*

D. R. Goodman, *Greed: A Confession: Poems*

Carrie Green, *Studies of Familiar Birds: Poems*

Margaret Ann Griffiths, *Grasshopper: The Poetry of M A Griffiths*

Janis Harrington, *How to Cut a Woman in Half: Poems*

Katie Hartsock, *Bed of Impatiens: Poems*

Elise Hempel, *Second Rain: Poems*

Jan D. Hodge, *Taking Shape: Carmina figurata;*
The Bard & Scheherazade Keep Company: Poems

Ellen Kaufman, *House Music: Poems; Double-Parked, with Tosca: Poems*

Len Krisak, *Say What You Will (Able Muse Book Award for Poetry)*

Emily Leithauser, *The Borrowed World (Able Muse Book Award for Poetry)*

Hailey Leithauser, *Saint Worm: Poems*

Carol Light, *Heaven from Steam: Poems*

Kate Light, *Character Shoes: Poems*

April Lindner, *This Bed Our Bodies Shaped: Poems*

Martin McGovern, *Bad Fame: Poems*

Jeredith Merrin, *Cup: Poems*

Richard Moore, *Selected Poems;*
 The Rule That Liberates: An Expanded Edition: Selected Essays

Richard Newman, *All the Wasted Beauty of the World: Poems*

Alfred Nicol, *Animal Psalms: Poems*

Deirdre O'Connor, *The Cupped Field (Able Muse Book Award for Poetry)*

Frank Osen, *Virtue, Big as Sin (Able Muse Book Award for Poetry)*

Alexander Pepple (Editor), *Able Muse Anthology;*
 Able Muse: A Review of Poetry, Prose & Art (semiannual, winter 2010 on)

James Pollock, *Sailing to Babylon: Poems*

Aaron Poochigian, *The Cosmic Purr: Poems; Manhattanite*
 (Able Muse Book Award for Poetry)

Tatiana Forero Puerta, *Cleaning the Ghost Room: Poems*

Jennifer Reeser, *Indigenous: Poems; Strong Feather: Poems*

John Ridland, *Sir Gawain and the Green Knight (Anonymous): Translation;*
 Pearl (Anonymous): Translation

Stephen Scaer, *Pumpkin Chucking: Poems*

Hollis Seamon, *Corporeality: Stories*

Ed Shacklee, *The Blind Loon: A Bestiary*

Carrie Shipers, *Cause for Concern (Able Muse Book Award for Poetry)*

Matthew Buckley Smith, *Dirge for an Imaginary World*
 (Able Muse Book Award for Poetry)

Susan de Sola, *Frozen Charlotte: Poems*

Barbara Ellen Sorensen, *Compositions of the Dead Playing Flutes: Poems*

Rebecca Starks, *Time Is Always Now: Poems; Fetch, Muse: Poems*

Sally Thomas, *Motherland: Poems*

Paulette Demers Turco (Editor), *The Powow River Poets Anthology II*

Rosemerry Wahtola Trommer, *Naked for Tea: Poems*

Wendy Videlock, *Slingshots and Love Plums: Poems;*
 The Dark Gnu and Other Poems; Nevertheless: Poems

Richard Wakefield, *A Vertical Mile: Poems; Terminal Park: Poems*

Gail White, *Asperity Street: Poems*

Chelsea Woodard, *Vellum: Poems*

Rob Wright, *Last Wishes: Poems*

www.ablemusepress.com